Theory Time!

Step by Step Instructions for ABRSM and Other Exams

Grade 2

by

DAVID TURNBULL

CONTENTS

Bosworth

THEORY TIME!

Grade 2

The purpose of these books is to teach the principles of music theory. They are intended not only for pupils who want to pass theory examinations, but also for all those who would like to learn something about the theory of music as part of their general education. This book covers the syllabus of Grade 2 of the Associated Board.

The sections of the book explain the ideas you need to know, and test your understanding with frequent questions. Write down your answers to these questions in the spaces provided, and then look up the printed answers

You will notice that answers to questions are always printed on different pages from the questions themselves. The answers to Page 1 questions are in the margin of Page 2, for example. Make sure that you look up printed answers *only* after you have written down your own, if you want to make good progress.

You can use this book with your teacher, who can set you pages to work through and then explain any difficulties you may have. Or you can use it to teach yourself, and you can use it for revision.

The sections of the book deal with different aspects of theory, but you need not work through to the end of each section before going on to the next. Your teacher may wish to recommend a different order of working – for example part of Section 1, then part of Section 2 before returning to complete Section 1. However, it is recommended that you should finish this book before you go on to Grade 3.

Extra practice can be had by using past examination papers published every year by the examining board, and from *Music Theory in Practice – Grade 2* by Eric Taylor, also published by the Associated Board of the Royal Schools of Music.

David Turnbull
Solihull, England, 1994

THEORY TIME! – GRADE 2

Section 1 - Time

Answers to questions on this page are in the margin of Page 2

Answers to Page 2 questions

Grade 2 times

1 In Grade 2 you need to know the Grade 1 times, $\frac{2}{4}$, $\frac{3}{4}$ and $\frac{4}{4}$, and also the new times of $\frac{2}{2}, \frac{3}{2}, \frac{4}{2}$ and $\frac{3}{8}$. All these times are called **simple** times – simple duple, simple triple and simple quadruple.

5(a) minim

(b) three

(c) minim

duple, triple and quad-ruple times

2 Duple time has two beats to the bar.

Triple time has three beats to the bar.

Quadruple time has four beats to the bar.

How many crotchet beats are there in each of the following bars?

(a) _____ 4 _____ (b) _____ 2 _____ (c) _____ 3 _____

6(a) $\frac{4}{2}$ - simple quad-ruple

(b) $\frac{3}{2}$ - simple triple

(c) $\frac{2}{2}$ or ¢ - simple duple or *alla breve*

time signa-tures with crotchet beats

3 In the time signature at the beginning of a piece of music, there are two numbers.

The top number tells us how *many* beats there are to the bar. The bottom figure tells us what *type* of note is used as the beat.

If 4 is the bottom number, it means that the beats are crotchets. 4 is chosen because four crotchets equal the length of a semibreve.

What are the time signatures in the bars in Paragraph 2 above?

7(a)

(a) _____ $\frac{4}{4}$ _____ (b) _____ $\frac{2}{4}$ _____ (c) _____ $\frac{3}{4}$ _____

(b)

time signa-tures with minim beats

4 The crotchet is often chosen as the beat, but any other note can be used instead.

If we use the **minim** as the beat instead of the crotchet, we cannot use 4 as the bottom figure of the time signature.

Instead of 4, we must use the number which shows how many minims equal the length of a semibreve.

How many minims are equal to the length of a semibreve? _____ 2 _____

9 quavers

5 If 2 is the bottom figure of a time signature, it shows that the beats are minims.

Complete the following:

(a) **²⁄₂** shows that there are two ___minim___ beats to the bar; ✓

(b) **³⁄₂** shows that there are ___three___ minim beats to the bar; ✓

(c) **⁴⁄₂** shows that there are four ___Minm___ beats to the bar. ✓

²⁄₂ or ¢ time
('alla breve')

6 **²⁄₂** is often called **alla breve** time, and the time signature may be written as **¢**

Write in the missing time signatures in the following bars. Underneath complete the name of the time (simple duple, triple etc.)

(a)   (b)   (c)

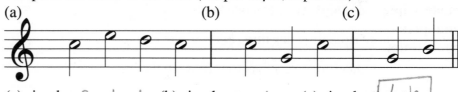

(a) simple ___quadruple___ (b) simple ___triple___ ✓ (c) simple ✓ | duple |

7 Look at these bars:

(a)   (b)

Bar (a) has 2 crotchet beats to the bar. Bar (b) has 2 minim beats to the bar. However, both bars will *sound* the same if the beats in both bars are played at the same tempo.

(a) Rewrite in **³⁄₂** time: ✓ (b) Rewrite in **⁴⁄₂** time: ✓

8 It is helpful to pencil in main beats over the tops of bars, and to put in dotted lines between the main beat divisions of the bars.

(a)   (b)   (c)

9 As main beats in **²⁄₂**, **³⁄₂** and **⁴⁄₂** are minims, half beats are crotchets.

What notes are quarter beats when main beats are minims? ___quavers___ ✓

2

**Answers to Page 4
questions**

14(a) beat 2
(b) a crotchet rest

**beaming in
times with
minim beats**

10 Beam quavers together up to the value of a minim beat.

Pencil in main beats, and beat divisions of these bars, then beam quavers together correctly.

(c) What note is one eighth of a beat when beats are minims?___Semiquaver

11 Mixed groups of quavers and semiquavers should be beamed together up to the value of a minim beat.

Pencil in main beats, and beat divisions, then beam correctly.

12 Rests may be included in beamed groups. Notice that the beam continues above or below the rest.

**completing
bars
i.
with notes**

13 You may be asked to complete bars by inserting notes. Look at the following example:

The time signature $\frac{3}{2}$ tells you that there should be three minim beats in each bar. The main beats have been put in over the top of the bars.

(a) Which beat is incomplete? _Beat 2_

(b) What single note would complete the beat?__a crotchet

Write in the note.

**ii.
with rests**

14 You may need to complete a bar by adding a rest or rests. Look at this example in $\frac{3}{2}$ time:

15
(a) 2 minim beats

(b) No

(c) Between bars 1 and 2

TEST 1 Answers
1(a)

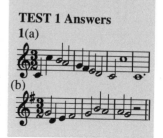

(b)

(a) Which beat is incomplete? _Beat 2_ ✓
(b) What rest will complete it? _crotchet_ ✓
(c) Insert it.

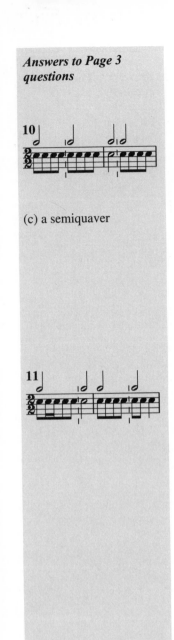

10

(c) a semiquaver

11

13(a) Beat 2
(b) a crotchet

rests of less than one beat

When you need to complete a beat with a rest:

(1) divide the beat into its two crotchet half beats;
(2) complete each half beat with any necessary rests, as shown below.

whole bar rests

In ²⁄₂ and ³⁄₂ time, a whole bar's rest is shown by a *semibreve* rest.

half bar rests

In ⁴⁄₂ time you may use a two beat rest in the first or second half of the bar, but *not* across the middle of the bar.

inserting bar lines

15 You will often need to put missing barlines into melodies. Look at this example, and work through the stages below:

Decide how many beats there are in a bar, and what note is used as the main beat.

a) How many beats, of what sort, are there? ___2 minim___ ✓

Draw the main beats over the bars in pencil, and dot in the divisions between the beats.

Start at the beginning, and count the beats until you get to where the first bar should end.

(b) Is there a bar line in place? ___NO___ If not, insert one. ✓

Count the beats until you get to where the second bar should end.

Continue in the same way until you get to the end.

(c) Between which bars did you need to insert barlines? _bars 1, 2_ ✓

**TEST 1
times with minim beats**

1 Insert any missing barlines in the following:
(a)   (b)

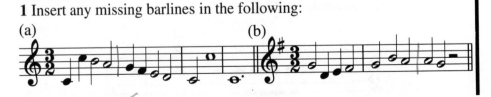

4

TEST 1 (continued)

2 Write in missing time signatures in the following:

(a) (b)

(c)

3 Complete these bars with a rest or rests at *

(a)   *   (b)   *   (c)   *   *

4 (a) Rewrite these bars in **4/4** time. (Pencil in the beats to help you.)

(b) Rewrite these bars in **2/4** time. (Pencil in the beats to help you.)

Write your score of correct answers here:_____If it was less than 8, read from the beginning again, and do the test once more.

19(a) complete
(b) incomplete
(c) third beat
(d) quaver note or rest
(e)

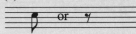

---

quavers as main beats

16 We have seen how minims can be used as the main beats. Quavers may also be used as main beats.

If we use the quaver as the beat instead of the crotchet or minim, we must choose a bottom figure for the time signature.

4 is the bottom number if crotchets are the beats, because 4 crotchets equal the length of a semibreve. 2 is the bottom number used if minims are the beats, because 2 minims equal the length of a semibreve.

What number must be used as the bottom number of a time signature which uses quaver beats? ____8____

3/8 time

17 In **3/8** time, there are three quaver beats to the bar.

Which answer is correct,

3/8 time is (a) simple duple time with quaver beats,
(b) simple triple time with quaver beats.
(c) simple quadruple time with quaver beats. *Answer:* b

21

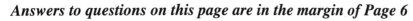

Answers to Page 5 questions

TEST 1 Answers (continued)

2(a) $\frac{3}{2}$ (b) $\frac{4}{2}$

(c) $\frac{2}{2}$ (or ₵)

3(a)

(b)

(c)

4(a)

4(b)

16 8, because 8 quavers are the same length as a semibreve.

17(b)

beaming of quavers and semiquavers

18 In $\frac{3}{8}$ time, you should

- beam the three quavers of the bar together;
- beam six semiquavers together;
- beam mixed groups of quavers and semiquavers together.

completion of bars in $\frac{3}{8}$ time

19 To complete bars in $\frac{3}{8}$ time with notes, rests or barlines, use the same methods as you used when the main beats were minims. Look at the examples below

There should be three quaver beats in each bar. The main beats have been put in over the top of the bars.

(a) Is the first bar complete or incomplete? ___complete___

(b) Is the second bar complete or incomplete? __incomplete__

(c) Which beat is missing? _3rd beat_

(d) What single note or rest would complete it? _quaver_ note or rest

(e) Write in the note or rest.

bar rest in $\frac{3}{8}$ time

20 Use a *semibreve* rest for a bar's rest.

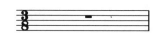

changing main beats

21 Sometimes you may wish to rewrite a passage using quaver main beats instead of crotchet main beats.

To rewrite this so that it is in $\frac{3}{8}$ instead of $\frac{3}{4}$, remember that in $\frac{3}{8}$ time single beats will be quavers instead of crotchets. Half beats will be semiquavers instead of quavers.

becomes

Both of these will sound the same, provided you play the main beats at the same tempo.

Rewrite these bars so that they are in $\frac{3}{4}$ time:

TEST 2
3/8 time

1 (a) Add a single note at * to complete these bars:

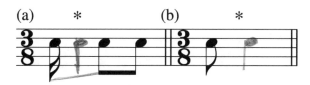

2 (a) Add a single rest at * to complete these bars:

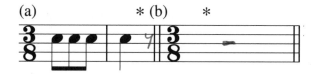

3 Add any barlines that are needed:

4 Rewrite these bars in notes of double the value:

Write your score here _____ If you made more than 2 mistakes, read 18-20 again, and do the test once more.

triplets

22 In all simple times, beats can be divided easily into two half beats. Crotchets can be divided into two quavers, minims can be divided into crotchets, quavers can be divided into semiquavers.

Sometimes, though, a composer needs to divide a main beat into *three* smaller notes instead of two. This is done by writing a **triplet.**

A triplet is a group of three notes which are played in the time of one beat.

The triplet has the figure 3 written over or under the notes, and the notes often have a slur as well.
Look at this phrase, in **3/4** time.

The first beats of bars 1 and 2 are divided into two quavers.

The first beat of bar 3 is a triplet - the three quavers must take only one beat.
What are each of the triplet quavers in bar 3 worth? __1/3 of a beat__

TEST 3 Answers

1(a) 3/2   (b) 4/4 or **C**
(c) 3/8

2(a)

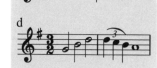

b

c

d

7

TEST 2 Answers

1(a)   (b)
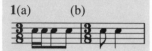

2(a)
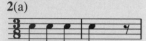

(b)

3(a)

(b)

4

23 Look at the following:

(1)   (2)   (3)

(1) Three triplet quavers are played in the time of a crotchet.

(2) Three triplet crotchets are played in the time of a minim.

(3) Three triplet semiquavers are played in the time of a quaver.

rests in triplets

24 You can include a rest in a triplet group. Notice that the beam is still used above or below the rest

TEST 3 triplets

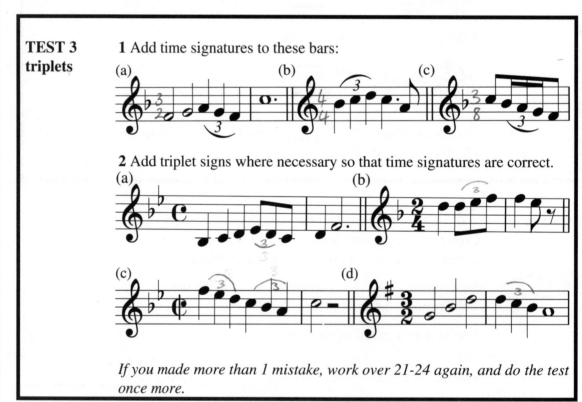

1 Add time signatures to these bars:

(a)   (b)   (c)

2 Add triplet signs where necessary so that time signatures are correct.

(a)   (b)

(c)   (d)

If you made more than 1 mistake, work over 21-24 again, and do the test once more.

22 One third of a beat.

*Answers to Page 10
questions*

Answers to questions on this page are in the margin of Page 10

1 In Grade 2, you need to know the notes of the treble and bass clefs, including notes which use up to two ledger lines above and below the staves. (Sometimes 'ledger' is spelled 'leger' – both are correct.)

treble clef

E G B D F

Revise the notes on lines in the treble clef that you learned for Grade 1.

Write under these notes their letter names, using sharp and flat signs where they are needed.

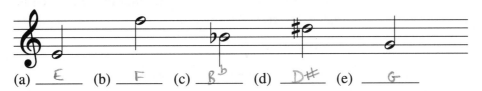

(a) ___E___ (b) ___F___ (c) ___B♭___ (d) ___D♯___ (e) ___G___

F A C E

Now revise the notes in spaces, and write under these notes their letter names:

(f) ___E___ (g) ___F___ (h) ___C___ (i) ___A♯___ (j) ___E♭___

6 F

bass clef

G B D F A

2 Revise the notes on the lines in the bass clef you learned for Grade 1 – they are in the margin.

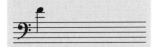

Write under these notes their letter names. Use sharp and flat signs if they are needed

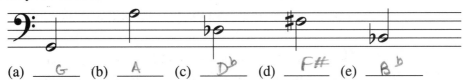

(a) ___G___ (b) ___A___ (c) ___D♭___ (d) ___F♯___ (e) ___B♭___

A C E G

Now revise the notes in spaces, and write under these notes their letter names:

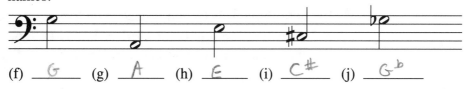

(f) ___G___ (g) ___A___ (h) ___E___ (i) ___C♯___ (j) ___G♭___

10 E

*Answers to Page 10
questions*

**middle C
on a
ledger line**

E   D   C

3 In both the treble and the bass clefs a ledger line is needed for middle C

In the treble clef, the lowest line of the stave carries the note E.

The note below E is D, and this is written immediately under the lowest stave line.

In order to draw middle C, the note below D, a ledger line must be drawn. Notice that

* the ledger line is only as long as is needed for the note.

* the space between the ledger line and the stave is the same as the space between the stave lines.

B   A

4 B is written under the C ledger line.

A, the note below B, is placed on a second ledger line below the stave.

Notice that this second ledger line is only necessary for A – you don't have to draw it under B.

A B C

5 In the bass clef, the note on the top line is A. The note above the top line is B. If you want to write middle C, you must draw a ledger line.

D   E

6 The note above middle C is D. If you want to write the E above it, draw a second ledger line for the E.

What is the name of the note above E? ___F___
Draw it as a crotchet.

7 By using ledger lines, you can now write all the notes between the top of the bass clef, and the bottom of the treble clef.

**ledger lines
above the
treble stave**

8 The top line of the treble clef carries the note F. G is the note immediately above F; it doesn't need a separate ledger line. A needs a ledger line and this ledger line is also needed for B.

F   G   A   B

9 The note above B is C, and it needs two ledger lines. The note above this second ledger line is D – the highest note you need to know in Grade 2.

B   C   D

**ledger lines
below the
bass stave**

10 Look at these bass clef notes. G and F are named. What is the name of the note on the ledger line? __E__

G   F

11 The second ledger line below the bass stave
carries the note C.
What are the names of the notes
(a) above it? __D__ (b) below it? __B__

TEST 4

1 Name the treble clef notes below:

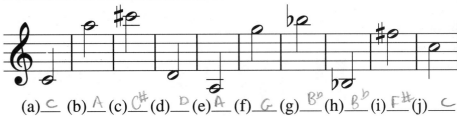

(a)__C__ (b)__A__ (c)__C#__ (d)__D__ (e)__A__ (f)__G__ (g)__B♭__ (h)__B♭__ (i)__F#__ (j)__C__

2 Name the bass clef notes below

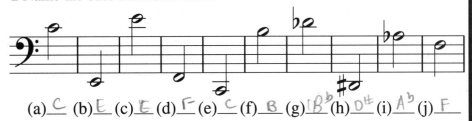

(a)__C__ (b)__E__ (c)__E__ (d)__F__ (e)__C__ (f)__B__ (g)__B♭__ (h)__D#__ (i)__A♭__ (j)__F__

3 Rewrite in the bass clef but at the same pitch:

4 Rewrite in the treble clef but at the same pitch:

5 Write in the clefs to make these the notes named:

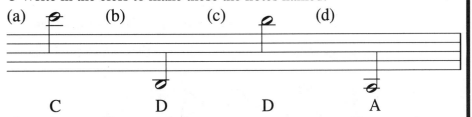

C   D   D   A

*Award yourself one mark for every correct answer. If you made more
than four mistakes, read from the beginning and do the test again.*

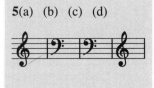
Answers to questions on this page are in the margin of Page 11

grade 2 scales

1 In Grade 2, you need to know the major scales of A, B flat and E flat as well as the Grade 1 major scales of C, G, D and F. You must also know the minor scales of A, E and D

intervals between notes of major scales

2 We can revise what was learned in Grade 1 by looking at the scale of C major:

The notes of the scale are called **degrees** of the scale and numbered from 1 to 7.

In C major, the first degree of the scale is C, the second degree is D and so on up to 7.
(Often in this book, the number alone is used, and the word degree is left out.)

Between the keynote C (1), and D (2) there is a **tone;**

Between D (2) and E (3) there is a **tone.**

What is the interval between E (3) and F (4)? ___Semitone___

3 Between F (4) and G (5) there is a **tone.**
Between G (5) and A (6) there is a **tone.**
Between A (6) and B (7) there is a **tone.**
What is the interval between B (7) and the top keynote? ___Semitone___

TTSTTTS

4 The intervals between the notes of C major, and all other major scales are therefore **Tone-Tone-Semitone-Tone-Tone-Tone-Semitone**. We can shorten these to TTSTTTS.

5 In C major, the pattern TTSTTTS can be found on white notes alone. All other major scales must use one or more black notes - either sharps, or flats.

These sharps or flats are shown in the **key signatures.**

Of which Grade 1 major scales are these the key signatures?

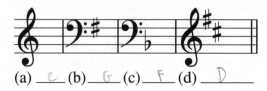

(a) __C__ (b) __G__ (c) __F__ (d) __D__

series of scales with sharps

6 C major has no sharps.

The scale starting on the fifth degree of C, G major, has one sharp.

D is the fifth degree of G major. D major has two sharps.

So we have a series of scales, each one in the series being five notes apart.

A major

7 The fifth degree of D major is A. Look at the keyboard below:

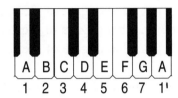

(a) What is the interval between A and B – tone or semitone? ____tone____

(b) What is the interval between B and C – tone or semitone? _semitone_

(c) What should the interval be between the second and third notes of a major scale to keep the TTSTTTS pattern? ____tone____

(d) What black note must be chosen instead of C? _C sharp_

The first three notes of A major are therefore A, B and C sharp.

8. The interval between C sharp (3) and D (4) is a **semitone**, which is correct.

The interval between D (4) and E (5) is a **tone,** which is correct.

However, E (5) to F is a semitone, and the interval between 5 and 6 should be a tone.

What black note is a tone higher than E? _F sharp_

9 (a) What is the interval between F sharp (6) and G? _Semitone_

(b) What is the interval between G and top A? ____tone____

To keep the TTSTTTS major scale pattern, we will need to choose G sharp as the 7th degree of A major.

F sharp (6) to G sharp (7) is a **tone**. G sharp (7) to top A is a **semitone**.

The scale of A major is shown below. Semitones are bracketed.

key signature of A major

10 The key signature of A major is three sharps – F sharp, C sharp and G sharp.

11 Notice the order in which the sharps appear. F sharp is written first because it is the first sharp to enter the series of scales with sharps. C sharp comes next, because it is the second sharp to enter the series of scales. G sharp comes last, because A major is its first appearance.

C major   G major   D major   A major

12 Look at the key signatures above.
(a) In G major, what degree of the scale is F sharp? _____
(b) In D major, what degree of the scale is C sharp? _____
(c) In A major, what degree of the scale is G sharp? _____

It is useful to remember that in a key signature of a major key with sharps, **the last sharp to the right is the seventh degree of the scale.**

**major
scales with
flats**

13 Now we can look at scales with flats in their key signatures.

Using the diagram of the keyboard to help you, count **down** five notes from C, including C in your counting.

What note is five notes below C? ____

14 We have already seen in Grade 1 work that F major has one flat, B flat.

To find the major scale which has two flats, look at the music below, and count down 5 notes from top F, including top F in your counting.

What note is five notes below top F? _____

15 If you count **down five notes** from a keynote, you get to the same degree of the scale as you do if you count **up four notes** from the keynote. Try this, using the F major scale in **14** above

If you *count down five notes* from top F on the line of music above you reach a B flat. If you *count up four notes* from the lower F you also reach a B flat.

Many people find it easier to count upwards rather than downwards – do whichever you prefer.

Answers (margin):
7(a) tone
(b) semitone

(c) a tone
(d) C sharp

8 F sharp

9(a) a semitone
(b) a tone

B flat major

16 Look at this diagram of the keyboard. B flat is marked for you.

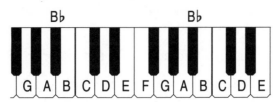

What are the intervals between (a) B flat (keynote) and C (2)_____;
(b) C (2) and D (3); _____ (c) D (3) and E? _____

The interval between the third and fourth degree of a major scale must be a *semitone* to keep the TTSTTTS pattern of the major scale. But D to E is a *tone*.

So E flat must be used instead of E. This will give a semitone between 3 and 4, and a tone between 4 and 5, which is correct.

No other black notes are needed until we reach the top keynote. F (5) to G (6) is a tone; G (6) to A (7) is a tone; A to top B flat is a semitone.

Two flats are needed therefore in the scale of B flat major: B flat and E flat. Here is the scale of B flat major without key signature.

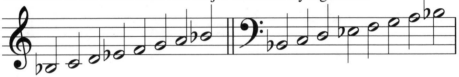

B flat major key signature

17 The key signature of B flat major is B flat and E flat.

Notice that the E flat used is the *upper* E flat of the two available in the treble clef.

18 F major, the first scale in the series of scales with flats in their key signatures, has one flat, B flat.

(a) Which degree of the scale is B flat in the scale of F?____

(b) In B flat major, the extra flat introduced is E flat. Which degree of the scale of B flat is the note E flat? ___

E flat major

19 The scale which has three flats will start on the note which is the fourth note of B flat major , We have found out in 18 that this fourth note is E flat.
Look at the diagram of the keyboard. E flat is marked for you.

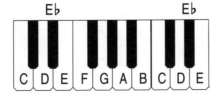

E flat (1) to F (2) is a **tone**. F (2) to G (3) is a **tone**. What is the interval between G (3) and A? _____

As G to A is a tone, and we need only a semitone, we will have to use A flat as the fourth note of the scale. This will keep the TT<u>S</u>TTTS pattern of a major scale.

The first four notes of E flat major are E flat, F, G and A flat.

The interval between the fourth and fifth notes of a major scale must be a tone. A flat to B is more than a tone - it is three semitones.

Therefore B flat must be used as the fifth note of E flat major.

B flat (5) to C (6) is a **tone**. C (6) to D (7) is a **tone**. D (7) to top E flat is a **semitone**. All these are correct.

The scale of E flat major, with semitones marked with brackets, is

The key signature has the flats in the order B flat, E flat and A flat.

16(a) a tone; (b) a tone; (c) a tone.

18(a) the fourth (b) the fourth

19 a tone

TEST 5

major scales

1 Of what major scales are these the key signatures?

(a)_____ (b) _____ (c)_____ (d) _____ (e) _____

(f) _____ (g) _____ (h) _____ (i) _____ (j) _____

2 Write out the scales named, without using key signatures, in the rhythms shown: Bracket semitones.

(a) E flat major descending   (b) B flat major ascending

3 Insert the necessary accidentals to make these the scales named:

(a) A major   (b) E flat major

Give yourself 1 mark for every completely correct answer. Write your score here ____ If it was less than 13, read over 1 to 19 again and do the test once more

MINOR SCALES

20 **Minor** scales and keys are as common as majors. In Grade 2, we have to know the scales of A minor, E minor and D minor.

There are two types of minor scales in use now. These are called the **melodic** minor scale and the **harmonic** minor scale.

Both types of modern minor scale are descended from an older form of minor scale, the *natural minor scale*, which we will always study first.

A minor

21

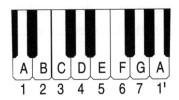

25 G sharp

Look at the white notes between A and A', on the diagram of the keyboard.
These white notes make up the natural minor scale of A.

intervals in natural minor scales

(a) What is the interval between A, the keynote, and B (2)? _____
(b) What is the interval between B (2) and C (3) _____
(c) What is interval between C (3) and D (4)? _____

So the first four notes of A natural minor scale have between them the intervals of a **tone**, a **semitone** and a **tone**.

The interval between D (4) and E (5) is a **tone**;

The interval between E (5) and F (6) is a **semitone**;
The interval between F (6) and G (7) is a t**one;**
The interval between G (7) and top A is a **tone**

TSTTSTT

A minor, and all other natural minor scales, have the intervals between their notes of **Tone - Semitone - Tone - Tone - Semitone - Tone - Tone.** We can shorten this to TSTTSTT

key signature of A minor

22 The key signature of a minor scale of *any* sort – natural minor, harmonic minor or melodic minor – is *always* taken from the notes of the natural minor scale, not from the melodic or harmonic forms.

As there are no sharps or flats in the scale of A natural minor, the key signature of all types of A minor is as shown on the left.

What *major* scale has the same key signature as A minor? _____

relative minors and majors

23 Because C major has the same key signature as A minor, we call C major the **relative major** of A minor. A minor is likewise the **relative minor** of C major.

A melodic minor

24 The **melodic** minor scale *when descending* uses the notes of the natural minor without any change.

A natural minor descending   A melodic minor descending

25 **When ascending, melodic minors sharpen the 6th and 7th degrees of the natural minor.**

In A melodic minor ascending, the 6th degree is F sharp. What is the 7th degree? _____

A natural minor ascending   A melodic minor ascending

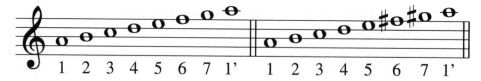

A melodic minor ascending and descending

21(a) a tone
(b) a semitone
(c) a tone

A harmonic minor

26 All **harmonic** minors **ascend and descend in the same way**. They use the notes of the natural minor, except that **the 7th degree is always sharpened.**

Remember when descending that notes are *numbered from the bottom keynote upwards.* So if you are writing a scale from the top keynote downwards, the 7th degree of the scale is one below the top.

A natural minor ascending   A natural minor descending

A harmonic minor ascending   A harmonic minor descending

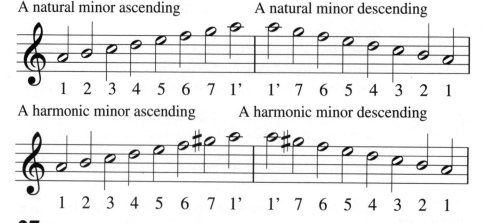

choice of minor scale

27 In Grade 2, you are allowed to choose **either** harmonic minor scales **or** melodic minor scales, but you must state which type of minor scale you are using.

TEST 6
A MINOR

1 Write A natural minor, ascending and descending in crotchets:

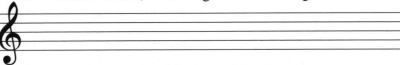

2 Name the relative major of the key of A minor _____

Either **3** Write in minims A melodic minor ascending and descending,
or **4** Write in minims A harmonic minor ascending and descending.

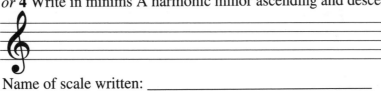

Name of scale written: _____

If you made more than one mistake, read over 20-27 again and do the test once more.

31

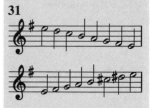

E natural minor

28 Look at the diagram of the keyboard below:

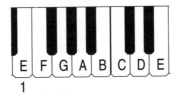

(a) What is the interval between the keynote E (1) and F? _____

(b) What is the correct interval between the first and second degrees of a natural minor scale? (TSTTSTT) _____

(c) What black note will have to be chosen as the second degree of E minor? _____

F sharp (2) to G (3) is a **semitone**; G (3) to A(4) is a **tone**; A (4) to B (5) is a **tone**; B(5) to C (6) is a **semitone**; C (6) to D (7) is a **tone**; D(7) to the top keynote E is a **tone**. All these intervals are correct.

32

29 The only black note needed in E natural minor, therefore, is F#

The key signature of E minor is in the left hand column. What major scale has the same key signature? _____

33 B flat

relationship of minors to relative majors

30 G major is the relative major of E minor; What is the relative minor of G major? _____

E is the sixth degree of the scale of G.

A minor is the relative minor of C major. The note A is the sixth degree of C major.

From these two examples, we can see that **the relative minor of a major scale starts on the sixth degree of the major scale.**

34 the sixth

19

TEST 6 Answers

2 C major

3

4

28(a) a semitone

(b) a tone

(c) F sharp

29 G major

30 E minor

E melodic minor

31 Remember that the melodic minor descends exactly as does the natural minor, but sharpens its sixth and seventh degrees ascending.

Look at E natural minor again in **29**, then write out in minims E melodic minor descending and ascending. Put in the key signature, and any necessary accidentals.

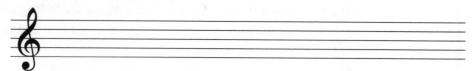

E harmonic minor

32 E harmonic minor ascends and descends like the natural minor, except that the seventh degree is *always* sharpened.

Insert the key signature and any necessary accidentals to make this the scale of E harmonic minor:

D natural minor

33 Look at the notes between D and the D above on the diagram of the key-board below:

Remember that the intervals between notes of a natural minor scale must be TSTTSTT.

D (1) to E (2) is a **tone**; E (2) to F (3) is a **semitone**; F (3) to G (4) is a **tone**; G (4) to A (5) is a **tone**. All these intervals are correct.

But A (5) to B (6) is a **tone**, although the interval between the fifth and sixth degrees of the natural minor scale must be a **semitone**.

What black note will have to be used instead of B? _____

B flat to C is a **tone,** and C to D is a **tone.** So the only black note needed in D natural minor is a B flat.

key signature of D minor

34 The key signature of D minor is B flat. The relative major scale which has the same key signature of B flat is F major. What degree in F major is the note D? _____

20

D melodic minor

35 The melodic minor descends exactly as does the natural minor, but sharpens its sixth and seventh degrees ascending.

Write out in minims D melodic minor descending and ascending. Put in the key signature, and any necessary accidentals, but remember that a flat, if sharpened by a semitone, becomes a natural.

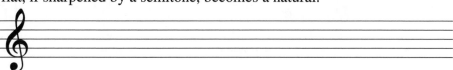

D harmonic minor

36 D harmonic minor ascends and descends like the natural minor, except that the seventh degree is always sharpened.

Insert the key signature and any necessary accidentals to make this the scale of D harmonic minor:

TEST 7 MINOR SCALES

1 Of what minor scales are these the key signatures?

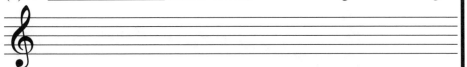

(a)_____ (b)_____ (c)_____ (d)_____ (e)_____

2 Write out the scales named, without using key signatures. You may choose whether you write out the harmonic or melodic minor, but must fill in the blank at * to show your choice.

(a) A*_____minor in crotchets ascending and descending

(b) E *_____ minor in minims descending and ascending.

3 Name the relative majors of (a) A minor;_____ D minor;_____
(c) E minor_____

4 These bars are in the key of D minor. Which degree of the scale is each of the numbered notes?

(1) _____ (2) _____ (3) _____

Give yourself 1 mark for every completely correct answer. Write your score here ____ If it was less than 13, read over 22 to 37 again and do the test once more.

38

1(a) C major / A minor
b. No
c. C major

2(a) F major/D minor
(b) C sharp
(c) minor
(d) D minor
(e) Yes - 7th

21

35

36

TEST 7 Answers
1(a) D minor (b) A minor (c) E minor (d) D minor (e) E minor
2(a) harmonic minor

2(a) melodic minor

2(b) harmonic minor

2(b) melodic minor

3(a) C major (b) F major (c) G major)

4(1) 1st (2) 6th (3) 7th

table of key signatures

37 Here are the key signatures of the scales with sharps which you have learned so far. Major scale keynotes are shown as semibreves; minor scale keynotes are shown as crotchets without stems.

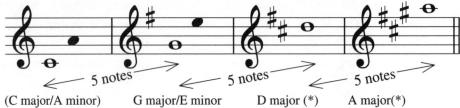

Here are the key signatures of C major of the scales with flats which you have learned so far.

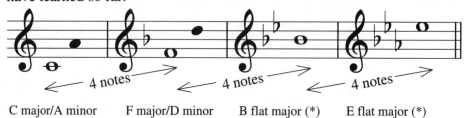

(* = relative minor not yet learned, as it is set for a later grade.)

naming the key of a phrase

38 You will often have to name the key of a phrase of music.

Use your table of keys in **37** to help you with this.

- Decide which two keys, major and relative minor, use the key signature of the phrase.

- If the key is major, there will be no accidentals in addition to the key signature.

- If the key is minor, sometimes the 6th and 7th notes of the key will be sharpened with accidentals.

Look at these examples:

1(a) What keys are suggested by the key signature? _____

(b) Are there any accidentals present as well as the key signature? ____

(c) What is the key? _____

2(a) What keys are suggested by the key signature? _____

(b) What accidental is present as well as the key signature? _____

c) Is the key therefore a major or a minor key? _____

(d) In which key, F major or D minor, is this phrase? _____

(e) Is the C sharp either the 6th or the 7th degree of D minor? _____

39 Name the keys of the following phrases:

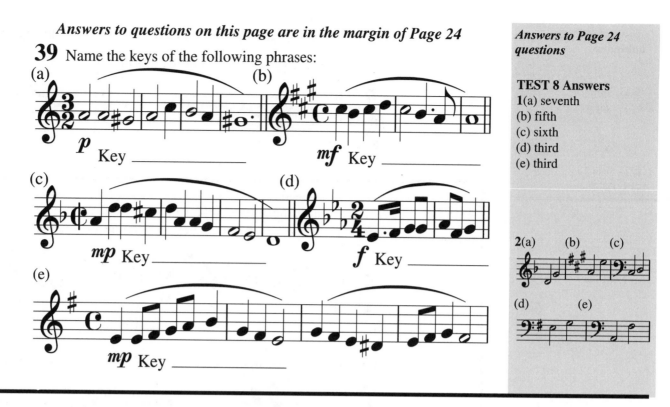

(a) *p* Key _____

(b) *mf* Key _____

(c) *mp* Key _____

(d) *f* Key _____

(e) *mp* Key _____

Section 4 – Intervals & Tonic Triads

---

intervals - revision of Grade 1 intervals

1 Read over the paragraphs on intervals in *Theory Time!* Grade 1.

The distance between two notes is called the **interval** between them. It is measured by counting from the bottom note to the top note, including the bottom and top notes in your counting. It is best to pencil in the notes between the bottom and top.

If the two notes of the interval are sounded at the same time, the interval is called a **harmonic** interval. If the second note is sounded after the first, the interval is called a **melodic** interval

The intervals set for Grade 1 were a second, a third, a fourth, a fifth, a sixth, a seventh and an octave in the keys of C, G, D and F majors.

These examples should remind you of your Grade 1 work. In each case the bottom note is the keynote.

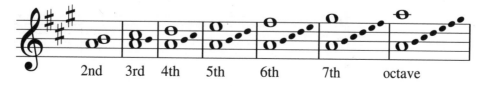

second (harmonic)   third (melodic)   fourth (harmonic)   fifth (melodic)

Grade 2 intervals

2 The same intervals need to be known for Grade 2 as for Grade 1 (see **1**, above). However, intervals will be set in the keys you have studied for Grade 2, as well as in the keys set for Grade 1.

Here are the harmonic intervals in the key of A major.

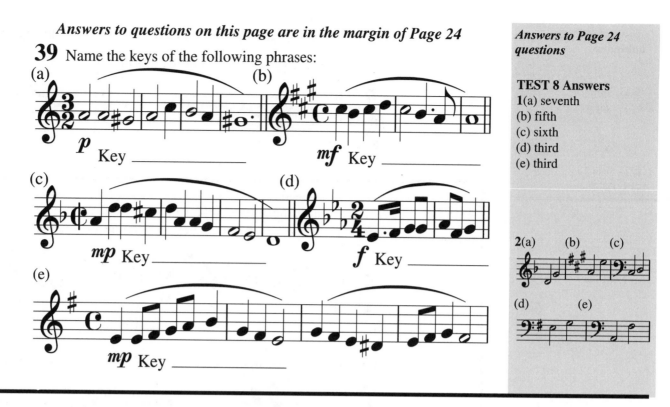

2nd   3rd   4th   5th   6th   7th   octave

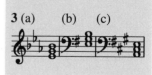

Answers to questions on this page are in the margin of Page 23

Here are the melodic intervals in the key of A minor.

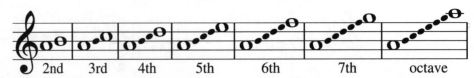

2nd   3rd   4th   5th   6th   7th   octave

TEST 8

intervals

1 Name these harmonic intervals. The bottom note is the keynote in each case. Pencil in the notes between the outside notes.

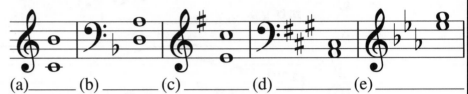

(a)_____ (b) _____ (c) _____ (d) _____ (e)_____

2 Write the following melodic intervals above the given keynotes:

(a) fourth   (b) seventh (c) second   (d) third   (e) sixth

Give yourself one mark for every correct answer. If you scored less than 8, read from the start of the section again and do the test once more.

tonic triads

3 The keynote of a scale is called the **tonic** of the scale. This note can be used as the bottom note of a chord of three notes. The other notes used are the third and fifth degrees of the scale.

To find the tonic triad of a key, write the key signature of the key on the stave, followed by the tonic. Then write above the tonic the third and the fifth degrees of the scale.

Notice that if the tonic is on a line the third will be on the line above, and the fifth two lines above. If the tonic is in a space, the third will be in the space above, and the fifth two spaces above.

tonic triad of: A major   B flat major   A minor   D minor

On the stave below, write the key signatures of the named keys, followed by the tonic triads:

(a) E flat major   (b) E minor   (c) A major

1 Only general advice can be given about composing. However, you should find that the following suggestions are helpful.

In Grade 2, you have to complete a four-bar rhythm of which the beginning is given. Phrases for completion will start on the first beat of the bar.

2 Try to write very simple rhythms, at least until you are really experienced. Remember that many of the greatest melodies are very simple indeed. *Always* tap over the rhythms as you compose.

Here is an opening to complete: [musical notation]

3 Add a second bar which balances the first bar. This can be as simple as a bar of crotchet beats. Or you could have two crotchets and a minim, or quavers and two crotchets.

[musical notation]   or   [musical notation]   or   [musical notation]

The rhythm will sound satisfying if the last part of the second bar has fairly long notes worth one or two beats.

4 Write the third bar. If your third bar is the same or very similar to the first bar, this will certainly sound acceptable. Here are some simple suggestions.

[musical notation]   or   [musical notation]   or   [musical notation]

5 The last bar of your four-bar phrase needs to sound final, and perhaps the easiest way to do this is to have a last note which is at least one beat long and preferably two beats long.

[musical notation]   or perhaps [musical notation]

6 Using rhythms composed above, you could write this as your finished rhythm,

[musical notation]

or this:

[musical notation]

to give only two possibilities. Experiment as much as you can.

7 You may be given an opening which is quite complicated in its rhythm. However complicated the start of the bar, try to complete it simply.

Suppose you are given an opening like this:

Complete the first bar in a really simple way:

then continue your phrase as shown in **1-5** above.

8 Keep a notebook of rhythms you like, whether they are written by you or by other composers.

9 Here are some other starts to phrases for you to complete:

(a)

(b)

(c)

(d)

(e)

(f)

(g)

(h)

(i)

(j)

(k)

Section 6 – Musical Terms and Signs

Answers to questions on this page are in the margin of Page 28

Answers to Page 28 questions

1 A list of musical terms and signs that you are expected to know is on Page 28. Those terms which are new in Grade 2 are <u>underlined</u>.

The musical terms are all in Italian, and you will need to memorise them with their English translations. However, you may find the follow-ing paragraphs make your learning of some of the terms and signs easier.

2 Number the following terms in order of speed, starting with 1 for the fastest and going to 7 for the slowest:

*andante*___   *allegro* ___   *largo* ___   *presto* ___   *grave* ___

*larghetto*___   *andantino* ___

3 Using your list of terms to help you, write down what you think the Italian words are which mean:

(a) very smoothly _____

(b) more movement _____

(c) getting a little faster gradually _____

(d) without getting slower _____

(e) sweetly and in a singing style _____

(a) $\frac{3}{2}$

(b) A minor

(c) F

(d) a natural

(e) a minim rest

4 Look at this phrase

Write or draw at

  (a) a tempo direction meaning fairly slow;

  (b) a direction showing that it is to be played expressively;

  (c) a marking to show that the notes in bars one and two are smoothly played;

  (d) an accent on the note;

  (e) a mark to show that the note is played *staccato*;

  (f) a sign over the last note to show that it is held on.

(f) *adagio* or *largo* or *lento*

(g) quiet and in a singing style

(h) 3 and 6

(i)

5 What are the meanings in English of

(a) *giocoso* _____   (b) *grazioso* _____

(c) *maestoso* _____   (d) *sostenuto* _____

Coda – fitting your knowledge together

Answers to questions on this page are in the margin of Page 27

Answers to Page 27 questions

2 presto - 1 allegro - 2 andantino - 3 andante - 4 larghetto - 5 largo - 6 grave - 7

3(a) molto legato

(b) *piu mosso*

(c) *poco accelerando*

(d) *senza rallentando* or *ritardando* or *ritenuto*

(e) *dolce e cantabile*

4
(a) *larghetto*

(b) *espressivo*

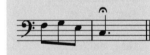

(*Coda* is the Italian word for a tailpiece – something played at the end of a piece of music.)

Now that you have come to the end of this book, you will be able to understand more about the pieces of music you play, sing, or compose yourself. .

See if you can answer the questions about this piece.*)*

*Dido's Lament:*Purcell

piano e cantabile

(a) Write in a suitable time signature in bar 1.

(b) In what key is the music? _____

(c) What is the letter name of the highest note of the piece? _____

(d) What is the first type of accidental which is written in bar 3?_____

(e) What is the missing rest in bar 9?_____

(f) What Italian word could be written which means the same as 'Slow' at the beginning? _____

(g) What do the words *piano e cantabile* mean underneath bar 1?

_____

(h) What degrees of the scale are the two notes in bar 6? _____

(i) Rewrite bars 1 to 3, and the first beat of bar 4 in $\frac{3}{4}$ time.

5(a) playful
(b) graceful
(c) majestic
(d) sustained

Musical Terms & Signs
(New terms for this grade are <u>underlined</u>)

Tempo:

a tempo	in time (*tempo* means time)
adagio	slow; leisurely
allegro	fairly fast
allegretto	fairly fast - less fast than *allegro*
andante	at moderate walking pace
<u>*andantino*</u>	a little faster than *andante*
<u>*grave*</u>	very slow and solemn
<u>*larghetto*</u>	fairly slow
<u>*largo*</u>	slow and dignified
lento	slow
moderato	at a moderate speed
<u>*presto*</u>	fast
<u>*vivace, vivo*</u>	fast and lively

Changes to Tempo

<u>*accelerando*</u>	getting faster gradually
<u>*allargando*</u>	broadening -slower
rallentando	getting slower gradually
(*rall.*)	getting slower gradually
ritardando	
(*ritard.*) (*rit.*)	holding back
ritenuto (*rit.*)	
<u>*tenuto* (*ten.*)</u>	held

Other

da capo (D.C.)	(repeat) from the beginning
dal segno (D.S.)	(repeat) from the sign, 𝄋
fine	end

Dynamics

forte (*f*)	loud
<u>*fp* (= *fortepiano*)</u>	loud, then immediately soft
fortissimo (*ff*)	very loud
mezzoforte (*mf*)	moderately loud
piano (*p*)	quiet
pianissimo (*pp*)	very quiet
mezzopiano (*mp*)	moderately quiet

Changes to Dynamics

crescendo (*cresc.*)	gradually getting louder
decrescendo (*decresc.*)	gradually getting quieter
diminuendo (*dim.*)	gradually getting quieter
<u>*sf* (or *sfz*) (*sforzato* **or** *sforzando*</u>	accented loudly

Manner of Performance

cantabile	in a singing style
<u>*dolce*</u>	sweetly
<u>*espressivo*</u>	expressively
<u>*giocoso*</u>	playful
<u>*grazioso*</u>	graceful
legato	smoothly
maestoso	majestic
<u>*moto, mosso*</u>	movement
<u>*sostenuto*</u>	sustained
staccato	sharp; detached

Qualifying words

<u>*Molto*</u> in front of a word means 'very', or 'much.' e.g.<u>*Molto piano*</u> means 'very quiet'. <u>*Meno*</u> means 'less. <u>*Piu*</u> means 'more'. <u>*Senza*</u> means 'without'. <u>*Con*</u> means 'with'. <u>*E*</u> or <u>*ed*</u> means 'and'. <u>*Non*</u> means 'not'.<u>*Troppo*</u> means 'too much'. *poco* in front of a word means little, or slightly. For example, *poco crescendo* means 'getting slightly louder'. <u>*assai*</u> means 'very'. <u>*simile*</u> means 'in the same way'. <u>*Al*</u> or <u>*alla*</u> mean 'in the manner of'' <u>*Ma*</u> means 'but'.

Signs

⎯⎯⎯⎯⎯ is often used for *crescendo*.   ⎯⎯⎯⎯⎯ is often used for *diminuendo*

A dot over or under a note, means that the note is to be played staccato. If a slur is written over staccato notes, they should be semi-staccato - not as sharp as ordinary staccato notes. A triangle means a very sharp staccato.

A > sign over or under a note means that the note must be accented. The sign ⌄ means an even stronger accent.

The sign ⌒ over or under a note means that the performer should pause on the note.

M.M. is short for Maelzel's Metronome. The performer is to set the metronome to the number which follows. If the direction is, for example MM ♩ = 60, it means that there should be sixty crotchet beats to the minute.

8va ⌐⌐⌐⌐⌐⌐⌐ · over a group of notes means that you must play the marked notes an octave higher . The sign *8va* ⌐⌐⌐⌐⌐⌐ written under notes means that the notes must be played an octave lower.

A slur over a group of notes means that the notes should be played *legato* - in other words, joined together. Don't confuse this sign with the tie, which links together two notes of the same pitch.

The marks at the end mean that you must go back to the first marks, and repeat the music between the marks.

Printed by
Halstan & Co. Ltd., Amersham, Bucks., England

10/05 (56498)